John Edwards Russell

Rational Horse Shoeing

John Edwards Russell

Rational Horse Shoeing

ISBN/EAN: 9783744662406

Printed in Europe, USA, Canada, Australia, Japan

Cover: Foto ©ninafisch / pixelio.de

More available books at **www.hansebooks.com**

THE VILLAGE BLACKSMITH.

RATIONAL

HORSE-SHOEING.

BY

WILDAIR.

WITH ILLUSTRATIONS.

NEW YORK:

PUBLISHED BY WYNKOOP AND HALLENBECK,

No. 113 Fulton Street.

1873.

INTRODUCTION.

IN presenting the observations contained in the following pages, we are aware that we appeal to practical men who judge by results, and have but slight patience with mere theory. We wish, therefore, to state clearly at the outset, that the system of horse-shoeing herein advocated, and the shoe offered by us to accompany it and accomplish its purpose, are the result of years of patient study of nature, and actual experiment; and that, although we have had to contend with ignorance and interest on the part of the farriers, and indifference and prejudice on the part of owners of horses, we have finally succeeded in interesting the most practical and capable men in

America, England, and France in the matter; and, at the time of this publication, thousands of horses, engaged in the most arduous labors of equine life—upon railways, express wagons, transfer companies, and other similar difficult positions—are traveling upon our shoes, their labors lightened by its assistance, their feet preserved in a natural, healthy state, and their lives prolonged to the profit of their owners and the advancement of that cause—one of the evidences of the progress of our age in true enlightenment—which has for its beneficent object the prevention of cruelty to the dumb and helpless companions of our toil.

GENERAL OBSERVATIONS.

THE first application of the Goodenough shoe is almost invariably to the feet of horses suffering from some one of the forms of foot disease, induced by the unnatural method of shoeing. Our system is intended for sound horses, to supply the necessary protection to the feet, and to keep them in a healthy condition. Our rules for shoeing, embodied in our circular of instructions, are applicable to sound horses, and disease must be provided for as exceptional.

Men are careless and, as a rule, unobservant; they go on in the old way until the horse flinches in action or stands " pointing " in dumb appeal to his owner, telling with mute but touching eloquence of his tight-ironed, feverish foot, the dead frog, and the insidious disease, soon to destroy the free action characteristic of health. It is when this evidence brings the truth home to'him that the neglectful **master,** eager to relieve the animal, tries our **system.** To such masters we must say, do not expect that **the impru-dence** and **neglect of** years can be **remedied** in an instant. The **age** of miracles **long ago** passed **away. We do not** propose **to' cure** by **formula, or bell and book.** There **is no** " laying on of hands "—no magical **touch of** an enchanter's wand.

Remember always that **pain** is **the warn-ing cry of a** faithful **sentinel on the outpost, that** disease is at hand. Disease is the punish-ment following a violation of the laws of nature, **and** can only be **escaped by** restoring natural conditions.

Remember **also, that "** Nature," **so** called by Hippocrates, **the** earliest systematic **writer upon** medicine, never **slumbers nor fails** in **duty, but** strives with unerring, **active** intelli-gence **to prevent** disease, **or to cure it** when it **can not be prevented.**

When the measures and processes of the **physician** are **in harmony** with the **natural intention, disease may be cured; when they** are adverse in application, the patient dies, or recovers in spite of art.

A great French philosopher powerfully remarked: "Nature fights with disease a battle to the death; a blind man armed with a club—that is, a physician—comes in to make peace between them. Failing in that, he lays about him with his club. If he happens to hit disease he kills disease; if he hits nature he kills nature."

We wish to be understood that in all things we would assist and facilitate the action of nature, under the artificial restraints of the horse. If we fail in this, or offer obstruction, our occupation is gone. The world has no time to listen to our theory, no use for our practice. And we hope that the thoughtful readers of these pages will see in our intention, an earnest, honest purpose and belief, and that, without affectation of science or pretense of superior knowledge, we base all our efforts upon nature and common sense.

In following our instructions and attempting to use our method, *have patience,* and note the result from day to day. The horse will

quickly tell you. His action will expose
quackery and unmask pretension. He will
be no party to a fraud, no advocate of an adver-
tisement.

SOUND HORSES.

A sound horse is, after man, the paragon
of animals. " In form and moving how express and admirable ! " His frame is perfect
mechanism, instinct with **glowing** life, and
guarded by the great conservative and healing powers of nature from disease and death.
His vitality is surpassed by that of man, because man has the endowment of soul, and in
his human breast hope springs eternal and
imagination **gives** fresh powers **of resist-**
ance. Like man, **the** horse conforms cheerfully **to all** climates and **to** all circumstances.
He is equally at home—

"Whether where equinoctial fervors glow
Or winter wraps the polar world in snow."

Amid the sands of Arabia his thin hide and
fine hair evidence his breeding; in the frozen
north **his** shaggy covering defends him from
the cold storms and searching winds. The

disadvantages under which he will work are in no way so clearly illustrated as in his efficiency when exposed to the evils of shoeing. Placed upon heel-calks, to slip about and catch with wrenching force in the interstices of city pavements, or loaded with iron-clogs, to give him "knee-action" and to "untie his shoulders," he bravely faces his discomforts and does to the best of his ability his master's will.

How quickly his active system responds to intelligent care and shows its beneficial results! And when relieved from the abuses of ignorance, his recuperative powers re-establish the springing step of youth.

CHAPTER I.

EVILS OF COMMON SHOEING.

EVERY horseman finds his chief difficulty in the fact that he has to protect the natural foot from the wear incident to the artificial condition in which the horse is placed in his relation to man. In those important industries where great numbers of horses are used, and the profit of the business depends upon the efficiency of the animal, the question becomes a very serious one, and the life term of the horse, or the proportion of the number of animals that are kept from their tasks by inability, make the difference between profit and loss to the great transportation lines that facilitate the busy current of city life. But notwithstanding the importance of this subject, upon the score equally of economy and humanity, the world is, for the most part, just where it was a thousand years ago, possibly worse off, for the original purpose of shoeing was only to protect the foot from attrition or chipping, and but little iron was used, but, as the utility of the operation became apparent, the smith boldly took the responsibility of altering the form of the hoof to suit his own unreasoning views, cutting away, as super-fluous, the sole and bars, paring the frog to a shapely smoothness, and then nailing on a broad, heavy piece of iron, covering not only the wall but a portion of the sole also, thus putting it out of the power of the horse to take a natural, elastic step.

In a short time the hoof, unbraced by the sole and bars, begins to contract, the action of the frog upon the ground, which in the nat-ural foot is threefold—acting as a cushion to receive the force of the blow and thus relieve the nerves and joints of the leg from concus-sion, opening and expanding the hoof by its upward pressure, quickening the circulation and thereby stimulating the natural secretions, —this all important part of the organization, without which there is no foot and no horse, becomes hard, dry, and useless. Then fol-lows the whole train of natural consequences. The delicate system of joints inclosed in the hoof feel the pressure of contraction, the knees bend forward in an attempt to relieve the contracted heel. In this action the use of the leg is partially lost. The horse endeavors to secure a new bearing, interferes in movement, or stands in uneasy torture.

Nature frequently seeks relief by bursting the dry and contracted shell, in what is known as quarter or toe crack, and the miserable victim becomes practically useless at an age when his powers should be in their prime.

Every horseman will acknowledge that his experience has a parallel in the picture here presented. Many men have at various times attempted reform, but the difficulty heretofore encountered has been that the mechanical application was in the hands, not of the owners and reasoners, but in those of a class of men who are, for the most part, ignorant, prejudiced, and, consequently, apt to oppose any innovation upon the old abuses in which they have had centuries of vested right; and it was not until the studies of Mr. R. A. Goodenough that there were brought to bear veterinary knowledge, mechanical skill, and inventive faculty, to overcome the stolidity and interest which have been the lions in the way of true reform.

CHAPTER II.

FROG PRESSURE.

THAT portion of the hoof called the "frog," performs the most important visible function in the economy of the movement of the horse. It is intensely vital and vigorous. The greater its exposure and the severer its exertion, the more strenuous is the action of nature to renew it. It is the spring at the immediate base of the leg, relieving the nervous system and joints from the shock of the concussion when the Race Horse thunders over the course, seeming in his powerful stride to shake the solid earth itself, and it gives the Trotter the elastic motion with which he sweeps over the ground noiseless upon its yielding spring, but, if shod with heavy iron, so that the frog does not reach the ground to perform its function, his hoofs beat the earth with a force like the hammers of the Cyclops.

With the facility to error characteristic of

14

the unreasoning, it has **been one of the** opin-
ions of grooms and farriers **that** this callous,
india-rubber-like substance would **wear away**
upon exposure to the action of the road **or**
pavement, and **it has been one** of their cherish-
ed practices to set the horse up upon iron, so
that he **could by no** possibility strike the frog
upon the ground.

In addition **to** this violation **of nature, they**
pare away **the** exfoliating growth **of the or-**
gan, and trim it into the shape that **suits**
their fancy.

Without **action, muscular life is impossible,**
the **portion** of the **body** thus situated must
die, paralyzed or withered. Motion, use, **are**
the **law** of life, and the frog of the horse's
hoof with a function as essential and well-de-
fined as any portion of his body is subject to
the general law. Without use **it** dries, har-
dens, **and** becomes **a** shelly excrescence upon
a foot, benumbed **by the** percussion of heavy
iron upon hard roads. This **is a** loss nature
struggles **in** vain to repair, the horse begins
to fail **at once.** The elastic **step,** which in a
state of nature spurned **the dull earth, becomes**

heavy and stiff, and the unhappy brute experiences the evils partially described in the previous chapter.

To restore the natural action of the foot by putting the bearing on the frog, is the chief object of the system we advocate, and the Goodenough shoe is designed especially to provide for that first and last necessity. If this is accomplished with a sound horse, he will avoid the thousand ills that arise from the usual method, and, so far as his feet are concerned, he will remain sound.

If the shoe is adopted as a cure for the unsoundness already manifested in animals that have been deprived of the proper use of their feet, it will cure them, not by any virtue in the iron itself, nor by any magic in its application, but simply by giving beneficent nature an opportunity to repair the ruin that the ignorance of man has wrought upon her perfect handiwork.

This part of our subject is so important that we shall return to it again in subsequent chapters, and enforce it at every point.

GOODENOUGH SHOE—FRONT.

CHAPTER III.

DESCRIPTION OF THE GOODENOUGH SHOE.

FROM the representation of the shoe in the cut, its peculiar conformation will be observed, and the reason for these changes from the common form we shall endeavor to explain as clearly as possible. In the first place, it is very light, scarcely half the weight of the average old-fashioned shoe. The foot surface is rolled with a true bevel, making that portion of the web which receives the bearing of the hoof, the width of the thickness of the wall or crust. This prevents pressure upon the sole, and makes the shoe a continuation of the wall of the foot. The ground surface of the shoe has also a true bevel, following the natural slope of the sole, and bringing the inner part of the shoe to a thin edge. The outer portion is thus a thick ridge, dentated, or cut out into cogs or calks, allowing the nail-heads to be countersunk. This arrangement gives five

calks—a wide toe-calk, the usual heel-calks,
and two calks, one on each side, midway
between the toe and heel—thus putting the
bearing equally upon all the parts of the
foot.

This calking has a double object. In the
common system of shoeing, to avoid slip-
ping in winter upon the ice, and in the cities
upon the wet, slimy surface of pavement, or
to assist draft, it is customary to weld a
calk upon the toe of a shoe, and to turn up
the heels to correspond. In this motion the
horse is placed upon a tripod, his weight being entirely upon three points of his foot, and
those not the parts intended to bear the shock
of travel or to sustain his weight. The posi-
tion of the frog is of course one of hopeless
inaction, and the motion of the unsupported
bones within the hoof produce inflammation at
the points of extreme pressure, so that, in case
of all old horses accustomed to go upon calks,
there is ulceration of the heels, in the form of
"corns," which the smith informs the owner
is the effect of *hard roads* bruising the heel
from the outside; he usually "cuts out the

corn," and puts on more iron in the form of a "bar shoe." Or the same action which produces corns, acting upon the dead, dry, unsupported frog and sole, breaks the arch of the foot so that a "drop sole" is manifest, or "pumiced foot," for both of which a "bar shoe" is the unvarying, pernicious prescription. In the Goodenough shoe, the calks are supplied, and the weight so distributed that the objection to the old method does not exist.

COUNTERSINKING THE NAILS.

This is a point to which we call attention as of great importance. In shoeing a horse for light or rapid work with a common flat shoe, seven or eight nail-heads protrude, and take the force of his blow on the ground. The foot has just been pared, and those nails, driven into the wall and pressing against the soft inside horn and sensitive laminæ, vibrate to the quick, and often cause the newly-shod horse to shrink, and show soreness in traveling for a day or two. No matter how skillfully shod, the horse will be all

the better in escaping this unnecessary inflic-
tion.

THE BEVEL OF THE FOOT SURFACE

Is to keep the shoe a continuation of the
crust or wall of the hoof, and to avoid percussion upon the sole.

THE BEVEL ON THE GROUND SURFACE

Is to follow the natural concavity of the foot
and to give it the form which will have no
suction on wet ground, will n t pick up mud,
or retain snow-balls.

THE CALKS

Have a use fully explained.

When the shoe thus described is set so as
to secure *frog pressure*, as hereinafter directed,
a horse may be shod without violation of
nature's laws; foot disease, under fair conditions, will become almost impossible, and the
useless refuse-stock, broken down by the old
method, may be restored to usefulness.

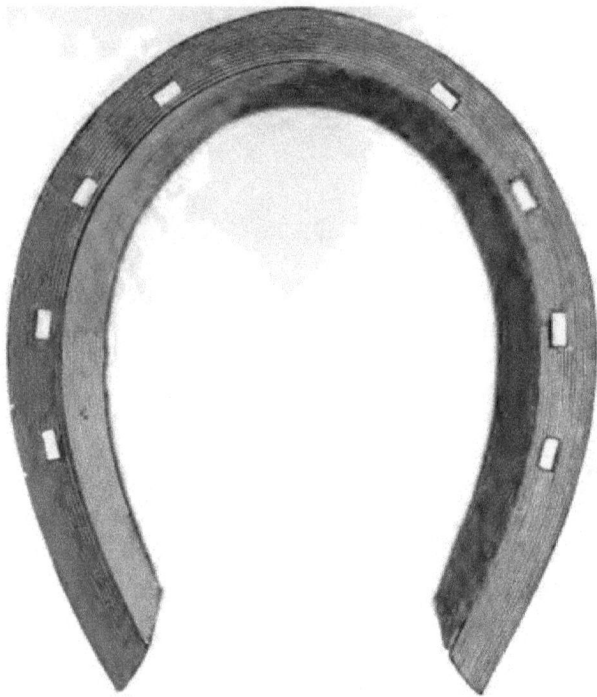

GOODENOUGH SHOE—BACK.

CHAPTER IV.

HOW TO SHOE SOUND FEET.

IF a foot came to the farrier in a perfectly normal condition, never having been subjected to the destructive process of common shoeing, the directions for putting on the Goodenough shoe would be simply, to dress the foot by paring or rasping the wall until a shoe of proper size laid upon the prepared crust would give an even bearing with the frog all over the foot; then, as the calk wore away, the pressure would come more and more upon the frog and the foot would retain its natural state during the life-time of the horse.

A colt thus shod could not have a corn, for a corn is an ulcer caused by the wings of the coffin-bone pressing upon a hard, unelastic substance. When the horse raises his foot the coffin-bone is lifted upward by the action of the flexor tendon; when his foot touches the earth the weight of the animal is thrown

21

upon the same bone, and, if unsupported by the natural cushion of the **foot, the** action of the bone pressing the sensitive sole upon iron causes the bruise which, for lack of another name, is called a corn. The horse thus shod would never have **a** quarter crack, for that is the **im-**mediate effect of contraction caused by **the** absence of the expanding action of the **frog** and the consequent dead condition of the **hoof** from want of circulation and proper secre-tions. The horse would be **equally** free from " drop " and " pumiced " sole, **seedy** toe, thrush, and kindred complaints.

INCIPIENT UNSOUNDNESS.

It is almost impossible to find a **horse** per-fectly **sound** in his feet, unless one looks (strange as it may seem) **into the** stables of the Third Avenue Railroad Company, or those **of** Adams' Express, or Dodd's Transfer Com-pany, or into **some** of the other stables where our shoe and system are in faithful use ; we will therefore call attention to such **a case as** will be generally presented at the forge : A good young horse, **shod** for several years

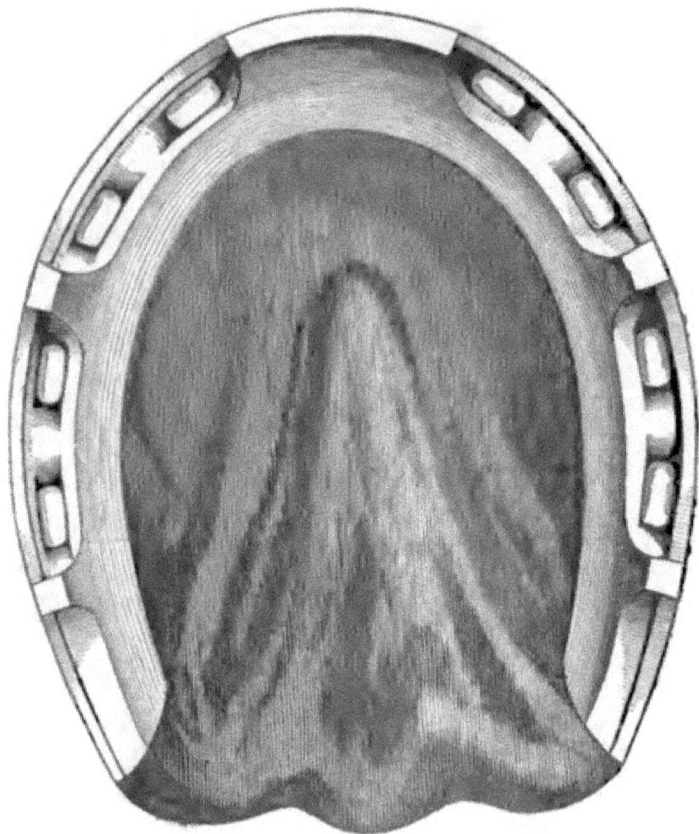

FOOT, SHOWING SHOE AND FROG.

upon the common plan, and in the early
stages of contraction. We find he has on
wide-web shoes, weighing about twenty
ounces each; these may be smooth in front
and calked behind ; they bear upon the sole
and heel. In place of a frog, we discover a
point of hard, shrunken. cracked substance,
neither frog nor sole. We cut the clenches
and take off the relic of ignorance and bar-
barism, throwing it with hearty good-will into the only place fit to receive it—the pile of
scrap-iron. We examine carefully to see
that no stub of nail is left in. The heels will
be found long and hard. Our object being
frog-pressure, to get the vivifying action of
this tactile organ upon the ground, we pare
down the whole wall; we soon come to signs
of a corn—perhaps a drop of blood starts; but
as we do not intend to put the weight upon
the heels, we are not alarmed. Having cut all
we can from the heels and still finding that
the frog, when the shoe is laid on, can not
touch the ground, *we knock down the last
two calks and draw the heel of the shoe thin;*
this must give us a bearing upon the frog

and the sound part of the foot. We use the lightest shoe, truly fitted with the rasp, not burned on. The horse should then be worked regularly, and he will experience at once the benefit of a return to "first principles" and natural action.

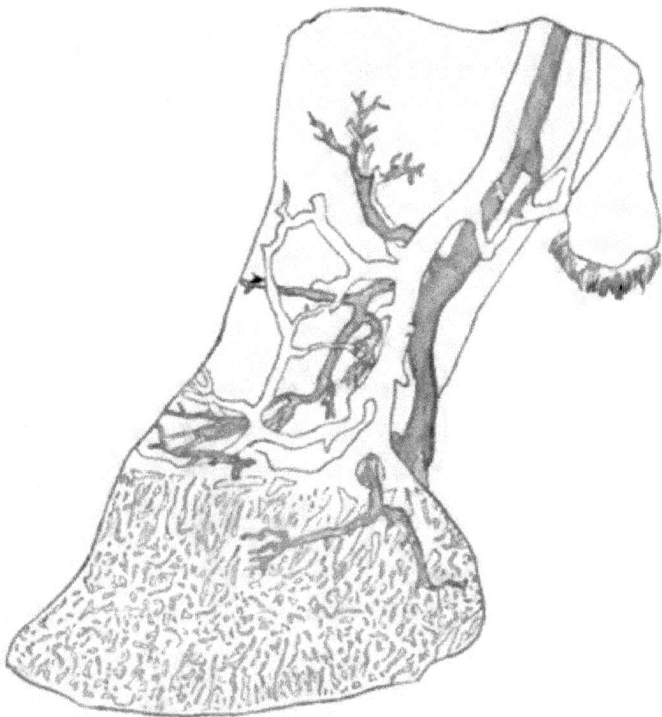

FOOT, WITH SHELL REMOVED.

CHAPTER V.

SIMPLE CASES OF CONTRACTION.

CONTRACTION, in a greater or less degree, is exhibited by all horses, of every grade, that have been shod in the common way, except in those more unfortunate cases that have resulted in a breaking of the arch of the foot, from lack of the natural frog support, when the phenomena of " dropped sole " are found, and the usual accompaniment of " pumiced feet."

It may seem superfluous to say that the power and action of the horse are greatly restricted by contraction.

The cartilaginous fibre that forms the bulk of the substance of the foot behind the great back sinew is squeezed into narrow space, the working of the joints compressed, and inflammation at the joints, or at the wings of the coffin-bone, is excited; in worse cases navicular disease is established, or, from inadequate circulation, thrush holds possession at the frog, or scratches torment the heels.   ·

When **simple** contraction—shown **in the** narrow heel, dried and shrunken frog, **and** " pegging " motion of the horse—is the **case,** **our** design is at once to restore the natural action of the foot. **This must** be done by expansion, and that is to be had from frog-pressure, according to the directions in the preceding chapters. **If navicular disease** has commenced, **and the** animal is decidedly lame, we have **a** difficult **case.** The membrane **of** this important **bone, in** some cases **of** contraction, **becomes** ulcerated, and the bone itself may **be** decayed, or adhesion **between** the coffin-bone and the navicular and pastern may take place. Without expansion there is no possibility **of relief;** local bleeding, poulticing, and all **the** drastic drugs of **the** veterinary will **be** invoked in vain.

QUARTER AND **TOE CRACK.**

This disease, usually attributed to " heat," " dry weather," " weak feet," etc., is one of

QUARTER CRACK—FULL SHOE.

the common symptoms of contraction, and can be entirely cured with the greatest ease; nor will it ever recur if the hoof is kept in proper condition.

If the case is recent, shoe as advised in our paragraph upon "Incipient Unsoundness," being sure to cut the heel well down, putting the bearing fully upon the frog and three-quarters of the foot. If the hoof is weak from long contraction and defective circulation, lower the heels and whole wall, until the frog comes well upon the ground, and shoe with a "slipper," or "tip," made by cutting off a light shoe just before the middle calk, drawing it down and lowering the toe-calk partially. This will seem dangerous to those who have not tried it, but it is not so. The horse may flinch a little at first, from his unaccustomed condition, and from the active life that will begin to stir in his dry, hard, and numb foot, but he will enjoy the change. The healing of the crack will be from the coronet down, and it is good practice to cut with a sharp knife just above the split, and to clean all dirt and dead substance out from the

point where you cut, downwards. Soaking
the feet in water will facilitate a cure by quickening the growth of the hoof; or, a stimulating liniment may be applied to the coronet, to
excite more active growth. Bear in mind
that expansion is not from the sole upwards,
but from the coronet downwards.

TOE CRACKS.

The cause of this defect is the same as in
quarter crack. It appears in both fore and
hind feet. Clean the crack well, cutting with
a sharp knife the dead horn from each side of
it; shoe as advised for quarter crack, or for
the purpose of getting expansion and natural
action of the dead, shelly hoof. The dirt and
sand may be kept out of the crack by filling
it with balsam of fir, or pine pitch. Keep the
horse at regular work.

QUARTER CRACK—HALF SHOE.

CHAPTER VI.

DROP SOLE AND PUMICED FOOT.

THIS miserable condition of the abused animal is Nature's fiercest protest against the ignorance and carelessness of man. A horse set upon heavy shoes, and those armed with calks at toe and heel, such as are usually inflicted upon large draft-horses, has his whole weight placed upon the unsupported sole. The frog never comes in contact with the earth in any way, inflammation of the sensitive frog and sole takes place, and the arch of the sole bends down under the pressure until the ground surface of the hoof becomes flat or convex, bulging down even lower than the cruel iron that clamps its edge. This is the condition of a drop sole. This degenerate state of the foot has other complications. Active inflammation is often present and all the wretchedness of a pumiced foot —the despair of owner and veterinary—is experienced. The smith, whose clumsy contriv-

ance has been the cause of all the woe, has
abundant reasons to offer for the disease,
and his unfailing resort of the "*Bar Shoe.*"
This atrocious fetter is supplemented with
leather pads, sometimes daubed with tar,
and the horse hobbles to his task. Not
unfrequently the **crust** at the front of the hoof
sinks in, adhering to the sole; circulation
being cut off,

SEEDY TOE

is then manifest.

The only possible relief from these complications is in natural action. Contraction is
not present, but we want circulation, new
growth and absorption; we obtain it by
dressing the foot smoothly with the rasp and
putting the bearing evenly upon the frog and
a light shoe, which should be merely a continuation of the wall of the foot. Many very
bad cases shod in this way have been relieved. No grease or tar should ever be
used.

CONTRACTION, OR DROP SOLE, WITH SORENESS AT THE TOE.

Shoe as previously directed, and rasp or cut the sole and wall at the toe into a slightly hollow shape, so that you could pass a knife-blade between the hoof and shoe. The object of this is to relieve the hoof from pressure at this point. In cases where the toe is thin and weak, or where there is inflammation extending to the point of the frog, remove as much of the sole pressing against the frog as seems feasible, and level the toe-calk, so that the horse will bear upon the frog and side-calks.

It is often well to free a shrunken frog from the binding growth of sole that has closed in upon it, and in cases of contraction, where this is done, a horse will recover the action of the frog with less difficulty than where that organ is sole-bound.

THRUSH.

This is a filthy, fetid disease of the frog. By many veterinary writers it is attributed entirely to damp stables, general nasty con-

dition of stall, yard, etc. Mayhew ingenu-
ously remarks, in addition, that it is usually
found in animals that " step short or go grog-
gily," and that the hoof is " hot and hard."
Youatt comes to the point at once in saying
that it is the effect of contraction, and, when
established, is also a cause of further contraction. It is manifest in a putrid discharge
from the frog. The matter is secreted by the
inner or sensible frog, excited to this morbid
condition by pressure of contraction. Its cure
is simple and easy if the cause is removed.
A wash of brine, or chloride of zinc, three
grains to the ounce of water, is generally used
to correct the foulness.

CHAPTER VII.

BENT KNEES INTERFERENCE. AND SPEEDY CUT.

THE knee of a horse is a most complicated and beautiful mechanical arrangement, singularly exempt from strain or disease in any form. Bony enlargement, inflammation of the ligaments, do not attack it. The ravage of the shoeing-smith—the horse's direst enemy—seems to be exhausted upon the feet and the sympathetic pasterns; the concussion of iron and pavement, uncushioned by the frog, will destroy the lower system of joints before the knee can be shaken.

Notwithstanding this perfection and strength, many horses bend the knee, and stand, or travel with it bent, until the flexor muscles shrink from lack of use. This "over in the knees" condition is invariably caused by imperfect use of the feet. The effect of heel-calks and their accompaniment of corns, making a sore in each heel, is often indicated by the horse to his regardless owner by bend-ing his knee.   The owner asks the smith why he does it, and the smith, who never fails to give a reason, says he has always noticed that horse had "weak knees."   We know of a shoer in Worcester County, Massachusetts, who has a wide local reputation for "doctoring" weak knees.   He holds that the muscles of the leg in such cases are *too short*, and have to be lengthened with thick iron heels and calks.   It is a favorite theory of this class of shoers that they are able to correct the errors of Providence in the horse's construction, and piece him out with heel-calks and bar-shoes!

INTERFERING AND SPEEDY CUT.

If horses were not shod, they would not interfere; it therefore follows that shoeing is the cause of this defect.   A contracted hoof, pain from corns, or any inflammation causes a horse to seek a new bearing.   In doing this he strikes himself.   Blacksmiths make "interfering shoes," welding side-pieces and superfluous calks upon their clumsy contrivances, and sometimes succeed in preventing the

symptom, but they never remove the cause.
Few horses with natural feet, good circulation, and shod with a light shoe, will ever
interfere.   In all such cases, take off the
heavy shoe, cure the contraction, get an even
bearing, and let nature have at least a momen-
tary chance.

WORKING UP HORSES.

It is a common practice of large proprie-
tors, engaged on railroad or city work, to buy
up horses with unsound feet, unfitted for speed
or gentle service, and use them up, as old
clothes are put through a shoddy-mill for
what wool there is left in them.   This cruel
policy, under an intelligent system of shoeing, would be impossible, because the vast ag-
gregate of foot diseases would be so abated
that horses, sound in general health but
creeping upon disabled hoofs, could not be
found in droves, as at present, and the specula-
tor in equine misfortune would better serve
his selfishness by buying young horses and
keeping them sound by a natural system of
shoeing.

STUMBLING HORSES.

This annoyance **is** frequently caused by undue use of the toe, when the heel is lame and sore from contraction and **corns**. When the horse has the frog well on the ground and uses his heel without shrinking he is not apt **to stumble**.

TO INCREASE COMFORT.

In dry weather, **or** when a horse with **a** hard, lifeless hoof is shod with the Goodenough shoe, and shrinks from the unaccustomed pressure of the frog on the ground, nothing is so grateful to his feet as cold water. The hose turned on them is a delicious bath; or if he can stand for an hour in a wet place, or in a running brook, he will get infinite comfort from it. We have sometimes **rapidly** assisted the cure of contraction, in the city, by manufacturing **a** country brook-bottom in this simple way: Put half a bushel of pebbles into a stout tub, with or without some sand, let them cover the bottom to the depth of two or three inches, pour on water and you have a good imitation of a mountain brook.

Put the horse's forefeet into this, and let him bear his weight upon the frog. The first time he will grow uneasy after a few minutes, but when his frog becomes natural in its function he will be glad to stand there all day.

Do not carry this treatment to excess. Moderation is the most satisfactory course in all things. Abjure utterly all oils and greasy hoof dressings, they are pernicious recommendations of unreasoning grooms. They fill the pores of the wall, and injure in every way. Nature will find oil, if you will allow circulation and secretion. through the action of the frog.

"Stuffing the feet," is another wretched, groom's device. A horse has a dry, feverish hoof from contraction, so his hollow sole, denuded of its frog, is " stuffed " with heating oil-meal, or nasty droppings of cows. When this sort of thing is proposed, remember *Punch's* advice to those about to be married, "Don't do it."

CHAPTER VIII.

ECONOMY OF THE GOODENOUGH SHOE.

A HORSE-SHOE that the united voices or the shrewdest and ablest managers in the country commend—inasmuch as it enables cripples to work, frequently restores them, and maintains soundness where that quality exists—need not be recommended on the ground of economy. Such a horse-shoe could not be dear. But it takes all sorts of people to make a world, and the pressure to the square inch of mean men is not to be governed by safety-valves or regulated by gauges. There are too many men who will use the thing that costs the least outlay, even if it tortures or kills the horse. On the point of first cost we may say that if our shoe had no advantage over the hand-made shoe in preserving the natural action and growth of the foot, thereby retaining the powers of the animal in full vigor, it would still be cheaper than the common shoe. It is sold slightly

higher than the clumsy pieces of bent iron
called horse-shoes by mere courtesy, and its
lightness gives one-third more shoes to the
keg, while there is no expense of calking,
which, in labor and material, is equal to
three cents per pound. Upon the point of
durability, it is well settled that the heavy
shoe will not last so long as the light one
with frog pressure. A horse set upon heavy
shoes grinds iron every time he moves. The
least interposition of the frog will reduce the
wear very materially, and if the frog is well
on the ground, a horse will carry a shoe until
he outgrows it.

A horse - railroad superintendent said to
the writer, "We don't wear iron nowadays,
we wear *frog* and *cobble-stones;* nature pro-
vides frog and Boston finds cobble-stones."
When the Goodenough shoe is put for the
first time upon a dry, half-dead foot, and the
frog brought into lively action, growth is
generally very rapid. We have often been
compelled to reset the shoe, cutting down the
wall, in ten days after shoeing. Many horses
that have been used upon pavements and

horse-railroads, have acquired a habit of slip-
ping and sliding along, catching with heel-
calks in the space between the stones; such
horses do not at once relinquish the habit,
and wear their first set of our shoes much
more rapidly than the subsequent set, after
they have assumed the natural action of their
feet. But, economical as a light shoe that will
long outlast a heavy one may be, the great
saving is in the item of horse-flesh.

The value of the horses employed in the
actual labor of the country reaches a start-
ling sum total.

The vast importance of the horse in the
movement of business, was never so fully
understood and deeply felt as during the year
past, when the epizoötic swept over the con-
tinent, paralyzing all movement and every
form of human industry. Even the ships
that whiten the seas would furl their sails
and steamers quench their fires but for the
labors of the horse. During the epidemic
the canal-boats waited idly for their patient tow-horses and railroads carried little
freight; the crops of the West lay in the

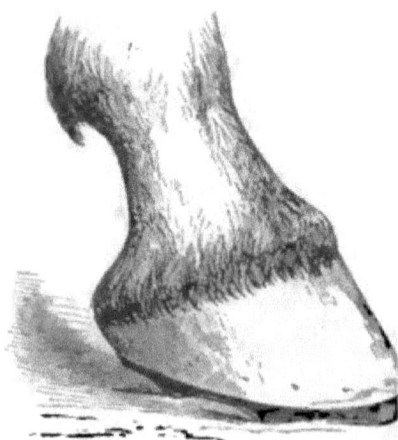

PERFECT SHOE AND HOOF

IMPERFECT SHOE AND HOOF.

farmers' granaries and the fabrics of the
Eastern loom and varied products of mechanical industry crowded the warehouses; even
the ragpicker in the streets suspended his
humble occupation, for the merchant, unable
to transport rags, refused to buy them of the
gatherer.   The investment of national wealth
in horses being so enormous, any means that
adds to the efficiency of the horse greatly en-
hances the general prosperity.

It is an old English saying, that "a good
horse will wear out two sets of feet."   The
meaning of this adage is obvious: a good
horse's feet are useless at the time when his
other powers are in the prime.   Mr. Edward
Cottam, of London, in his "Observations
upon the Goodenough System," states that
London omnibus-owners use up a young
horse in four years; that is, a horse of seven
years of age goes to the knackers at eleven,
pabulum Acherontis; and the only noticeable
cause of their failure is from diseases of the
feet.   A horse properly shod and cared for
should endure five times as long.   In this
country horses fail in the feet, and are called

old at an age when **they** should be **in the** fullest activity. This **is** a double loss, for every horseman of experience knows that if an old horse is sound and vigorous he has some great advantages over a young one. He is safer in every respect, " way-wise," seasoned, steady, and reliable. He and his **owner** are old friends and companions and **can not** part but with **a pang** of regret. A **good** horse, **well cared for, should work** cheerfully until he is thirty **years of** age; **yet how few are able** to perform genteel service after fifteen! **It is a** sad sight that of the high-mettled, noble animal, once the petted darling of wealth, caressed by ladies **and children,** and guarded so that even the winds **of heaven** might not visit him **too roughly, fallen through** the successive grades **of equine** degradation, until at last he hobbles before a clam-**wagon** or a swill-cart—a sorry **relic** of better **days.**

The question is so plain that we hesitate to argue with intelligent people to prove that, if the old system of shoeing destroys the **value** of a horse in middle life, half his money **value**

is sacrificed to ignorance—a waste that might be saved were nature's laws regarded. That part of the argument which demands that the faithful, devoted servant merits humane treatment and the best intelligence of the master in securing his health and comfort can not be forgotten and need not be urged upon the attention of the true horseman.

FINAL OBSERVATIONS.

TO be *rational* in any course of action is, primarily, to follow the leading of reason, and by that guidance to arrive at correct conclusions.

It is the opposite to the method which is *irrational*—regardless of reason, and therefore leading to conclusions erroneous and absurd. Rationalism is opposed to ultraism, to vehement, officious and extreme measures—while it would seek more excellent ways, it holds fast to that which is good.

Rationalism in medicine is the method which recognises nature as the great agent in the cure of disease, and employs art as an auxiliary to be resorted to when useful or necessary, and avoided when prejudicial.

In our treatment of the hoof, we would seek to know the cause of the horse's troubles, firmly believing that he is endowed by nature with strength to perform the service man demands of him, and that he is not necessarily a helpless prey to torturing diseases of the minor organs; and, indeed, subject only to that final, unavoidable sentence, which in some form nature holds suspended over all animate existence.

Having by the aid of reason ascertained the cause of defects, we would assist nature to relieve them; we have therefore called this little hand-book of suggestions from our experience, RATIONAL HORSE-SHOEING.

OPPOSING FORCES.

Having taken upon ourselves to reform evils, rooted deep in old customs, and to abolish abuses older than our civilization, we have to meet with discouragement and opposition in various forms.

Even the enlightened and well-intentioned hold back incredulous. This form of opposition finally examines, being led thereto from motives of economy and the promptings of humanity; it usually approves and assists, but is often carried back by indolence, when it discovers **that it** must join us in the loud battle we are forced to wage all along the line against fierce interests and bitter prejudices.

We attack with slender array, but unflinching purpose, the gloomy powers of ignorance **that** are allied **to** doubt and indifference. **These** contend under the prestige of a thousand years of possession.

Ignorance and Prejudice are twin giants **that** renew their life upon each other; they **are** as old as chaos, and are invulnerable to the weapons **of** ordinary warfare. Like the fallen angels, they are—

> " Vital in every part,
> And can but by annihilation die."

One of the Greek fables, typifying the struggle of man against circumstances, was a story of the battle between Hercules and Antæus, son of the Earth. The fight was long and doubtful, for whenever the mortal was felled to the ground by the power of the vigorous god, his force was renewed by **con**-tact with the breast of his mother Earth, **and**

he sprang to his feet and recommenced the never-ending strife.

This contest between the god, and the mortal born of earth and sea, is the poetical type of the unceasing toil of man in the Valley of the Nile, against the sandy waves of the Lybian desert, always encroaching upon the cultivated soil, and demanding year by year new exertions to repress their advance.

So, in our attempt to establish a better system of utilizing the powers of the horse in the service of man, we have each day to meet the same enemy, renewed by contact with the sources that foster and reinforce ignorance. But as persistent labor conducted the beneficent waters of the Nile in irrigating channels through the arid plain of the desert, until upon the inhospitable edge gardens bloomed, fields of grain waved in the breeze, and the date-palm cast its grateful shade upon the husbandman—so we make healthful progress, and enjoy a widely increasing triple reward—first, in the thankful esteem of our fellow men; secondly, in the relief we afford to a noble animal ; and last, in the substantial return

which the highest authority **has adjudged to**
honest labor.

REGULAR WORK.

We **wish all** readers of this book to under-
stand that the directions **herein given for**
shoeing apply to horses whose **owners** expect
them to work regularly **after shoeing—from**
the very hour in which the shoes are set.

We do **not propose to "lay** up**" horses, or**
to put them **to rest** in **"loose boxes," nor yet**
to "turn them out to grass.**" One of the**
chief difficulties we have had with wealthy
owners has been from the tendency to **keep**
the horse *out of work* when we have **got him**
into a condition **where we want** exercise to
stimulate the alterative process we propose.

A **cure of any foot** disease we have described, will **be much more** rapidly effected if the
horse has his regular work upon the roads or
pavements to which he **is** accustomed, no
matter how hard they are.

We hope that it **has also** been noticed, that
we **do** not propose to cure spavins, splints,

navicular disease, or to restore the natural action of a horse where ossification of cartilage is well established.